Foundations for Teens: A Study in the Book of John

Copyright © 2018 by FamiliesAlive®.
All rights reserved.
Printed in the United States of America.

No portion of this book may be reproduced in any form without permission from the publisher, except as permitted by U.S. copyright law.

For information, address:
FamiliesAlive®
PO Box 3288
Parker, CO 80134
www.familiesalive.org

First edition.

Cover design: Laura Cooper

Library of Congress Cataloging-in-Publication Data has been applied for.

ISBN: 978-1-946853-02-8

10   9   8   7   6   5   4   3   2   1

foundations FOR TEENS

By familiesALIVE®

Written by Becky Shultz
Edited by Laura Cooper

A Note to Youth Leaders

This book is dedicated to the next generation, and to all those committed to helping them grow into people of faith.

We believe that the teen years are critical for faith development, and that so many of our young people do not have an adequate understanding of the Gospel message.

That's why we developed the **Foundations for Teens** series – if nothing else, we want your teens to know who Jesus is, why He came to earth, why His death and resurrection are significant, and how they can respond to this life-changing news. Using the Gospel of John, this study will help teens discover these answers for themselves.

This workbook contains 14 lessons. When done once a week, this study takes about a semester to work through.

Each lesson includes a time of prayer, a Scripture passage from the Gospel of John, a place to journal, some comprehension questions, and a "so what?" reflection. When using this with a group, we recommend starting in prayer together, then silently working through the reading and the questions individually, then coming back together to discuss and dig deeper.

We hope that the students you lead will come to know the Lord more, love Him more, and serve Him more as a result.

Visit us at **www.familiesalive.org** for more encouragement and resources.

Becky Shultz
Community Engagement Director, FamiliesAlive®

TABLE of CONTENTS

Part 1: Who is Jesus?..5

Part 2: Why did Jesus Come?..................................21

Part 3: How do I Respond?......................................29

Lesson 1: Who is Jesus?

Pray

Jesus, please show me through your Word today who you are. Fill me with thoughts of you only, right now. I want to know you.

Read

John 1 *(Optional: Revelation 5)*

Write

Journal anything that speaks to you or jumps out at you from the passage, including any questions you might have.

_____
_____
_____
_____
_____
_____
_____
_____

Answer

Note: The Gospel of John was most likely written by Jesus' disciple, John, the one who refers to himself as "the disciple whom Jesus loved" (NOT John the Baptist who testified about Jesus, preparing the way for the Lord).

1) Look closely at the passage again. Who does John say Jesus was? For example, Verse 1 mentions that Jesus is the Word and the Word was God. So, Jesus is the Word *and* He is God. John says Jesus is many things. Find as many as you can.

2) What was made through Jesus (vs. 3)?

3) As the Lamb of God, what does Jesus do (vs. 29)?

4) If we believe in the name of Jesus, what right do we have (vs. 12)?

Reflect

This passage of Scripture tells us so much about who Jesus is. It is rich and vast, pointing to the One who is the Word, who is God, who is the giver of life, who is light, who is Lord, who is the Lamb of God, who is God's Chosen One, who is Rabbi (Teacher), who is the Messiah, who is the Son of God and the Son of Man (fully God and fully man, at the same time!), who is the King of Israel.

How could Jesus be at the beginning of time, creating all things? Because He is God! He is also the Lamb of God, come to us to take away the sin of the world. If we believe this, if our hearts cry YES and AMEN! Jesus is God, He is the Lamb who has come to take away my sin, then we are given a gift. We become children of God. May you know today that you are His. May you join all of heaven today in singing His praises. Worthy is the Lamb!

Lesson 2: Who is Jesus?

Pray

Jesus, please show me through your Word today who you are. Fill me with thoughts of you only, right now. I want to know you.

Read

John 4:1-26,39-42; John 6:1-35

Write

Journal anything that speaks to you or jumps out at you from the passage, including any questions you might have.

_____
_____
_____
_____
_____
_____
_____
_____
_____

Answer

1) Who does Jesus say He is to the Samaritan woman? (4:10)

2) Who else does Jesus say He is to the Samaritan woman? (4:25, 26)

3) Jesus stayed with the Samaritans for a time. Who did they come to know Him as? (4:42)

4) Who does Jesus say He is when speaking to the crowd of people? (6:35)

Reflect

Our bodies need bread and water in order to live. So it is with our souls. Our souls hunger and thirst for something. We try to satisfy our hunger and quench our thirst with all sorts of things – money, more stuff, fun, vacations, devices, social media, acceptance, popularity, praise, justice, independence, peace, healing (the list goes on and on). None of these things (apart from Christ) can ever satisfy and quench. The something our souls hunger and thirst for is Jesus. He is the only thing that can truly satisfy our hunger and quench our thirst. Jesus is the Living Water and the Bread of Life. Come to Him – and you will hunger and thirst no more.

Lesson 3: Who is Jesus?

Pray

Jesus, please show me through your Word today who you are. Fill me with thoughts of you only, right now. I want to know you.

Read

John 1:1-9; John 8:1-12; John 9:1-39

Write

Journal anything that speaks to you or jumps out at you from the passage, including any questions you might have.

_____

_____

_____

_____

_____

_____

_____

_____

Answer

1) Who is Jesus? (1:4-9)

2) As the Light, what does Jesus do? (1:5)

3) After speaking clearly against condemnation, who does Jesus say He is? (8:12)

4) What did Jesus do for the blind man?

5) What was the man's response, because of what Jesus had done for him? (9:38)

Reflect

If you go back to the very beginning of our world, to Day 1 of creation, Jesus was there. In all of His God-ness, He was with the Father, creating all things. Do you know what He spoke into creation first, before anything else?

Let there be light.

He spoke light into creation. I find that fascinating. The very first thing spoken into creation by Jesus is the very essence of who Jesus is. He is Light. He is the Light of the World come to shine in the darkness. He is the Light of the World come to lead us out of darkness and into life. He is the Light of the World come not to condemn, yet, somehow, to shine light on our sin, making us aware of it, calling us out of it. Just like He did for the woman caught in adultery. He is the Light of the World come to open the eyes of the blind, so that we may see clearly who He is. So that we, like the healed blind man, will believe that Jesus is who He says He is, and we will worship Him. May we know Him as the Light of the World, and may we come out of the darkness into His wonderful light (1 Peter 2:9)!

Lesson 4: Who is Jesus?

Pray

Jesus, please show me through your Word today who you are. Fill me with thoughts of you only, right now. I want to know you.

Read

John 10

Write

Journal anything that speaks to you or jumps out at you from the passage, including any questions you might have.

_____

_____

_____

_____

_____

_____

_____

_____

Answer

1) Who does Jesus say He is? (vs. 7)

2) Why has Jesus come? (vs. 10)

3) Who does Jesus say He is? (vs. 11)

4) What does the good shepherd do for His sheep?

5) What are we given when we listen to His voice and follow Him?

Reflect

Have you ever been on a farm or a ranch? If so, you will notice fencing all around. Why? Well, in order to keep the animals in, to keep the animals where they are supposed to be, to keep the animals safe, fences surround them. The only right way to enter those fences is through the gate.

Jesus makes clear that He is the gate for His sheep. There is only one way to the Father, only one way to safety, only one way to where we are supposed to be. That way is through the gate. That way is through Jesus.

He also makes clear that He is the Good Shepherd. Shepherds are known for meeting the needs of their sheep. They are known for tirelessly searching for sheep that have wandered away from the fold. They are known for protecting their sheep from predators. They are known for firmly keeping their sheep on the right path. They are known for their tender, loving care. Jesus meets our needs. He tirelessly searches for us when we wander. He protects us. He keeps us on the right path. He tenderly cares for us, loving us with an astounding, everlasting love!

But, Jesus does not stop there. He takes His love even further for us, His sheep. As the Good Shepherd, Jesus lays down His life for us.

May we boldly walk through The Gate, declaring that Jesus is the only way. May we enjoy the abundant life that only He can give (vs. 10). May we listen to His voice and follow Him, knowing that we rest safely in the palm of our good Father's hand (vs. 28, 29). May we embrace the freedom that comes from knowing our Shep-herd gave His life so that we might live.

Lesson 5: Who is Jesus?

Pray

Jesus, please show me through your Word today who you are. Fill me with thoughts of you only, right now. I want to know you.

Read

John 14:1-11

Write

Journal anything that speaks to you or jumps out at you from the passage, including any questions you might have.

_____
_____
_____
_____
_____
_____
_____
_____

Answer

1) Who does Jesus say He is? (vs. 6)

2) How do we come to the Father? (vs. 6)

3) If we know Jesus, who else do we know? (vs. 7)

4) Jesus was planning to leave. What has He been doing ever since? (vs. 2-3)

Reflect

We live in a day and age when anything goes. Our culture says that what is truth for you might not be truth for me. It tells us that there are many ways to heaven. It doesn't matter what you believe in, as long as you believe in something. This is absolutely a lie from the Deceiver himself. He wants nothing better than to steer us clear of the Way, the Truth, the Life.

God's Word is *true*. It has endured the test of time. It has been proven over and over again. He has been proven over and over again. There is only one way to the Father, only one way to heaven. That way is Jesus. There is only one truth – one who always speaks the truth, one we can completely rely on. That truth is Jesus. There is only one life. One who created all things. One who can give us eternal (forever) life. That life is Jesus.

Jesus is the WAY, the TRUTH, and the LIFE. May we follow Him. May we believe His every word. May we open our hands and our hearts to the life He has for us here and the life He's preparing for us there.

Lesson 6: Who is Jesus?

Pray

Jesus, please show me through your Word today who you are. Fill me with thoughts of you only, right now. I want to know you.

Read

John 15:1-11

Write

Journal anything that speaks to you or jumps out at you from the passage, including any questions you might have.

_____
_____
_____
_____
_____
_____
_____
_____

Answer

1) Who does Jesus say He is?

2) How do we bear fruit? (vs. 4-5)

3) What good comes from bearing much fruit? (vs. 8)

4) Why does Jesus say to remain in His love and obey His commands? (vs. 9-11)

Reflect

If you have never seen a grapevine, do a quick internet search. Find images of vines that are fruitful, and images of vines that are dead. What you will notice is that a fruit-ful vine has branches which bear fruit. Those branches are beautiful, producing glorious fruit. The branches which do not bear fruit are withered and hideous.

Here's what else you'll notice: Those fruitful branches are not just hanging out by themselves. They are all connected to the vine. If you were in charge of a vineyard, if your livelihood came from the fruitfulness of that vineyard, you would never cut off fruit-bearing branches from the vine. Why not? Because those branches (even if they are lush and beautiful and fruitful at the time you cut them away) would shrivel up and die. Apart from the vine, they can bear no fruit!

So it is with you and with me. Apart from Jesus, we are not capable of much. In fact, apart from Him we can do nothing. Jesus is the vine. We are the branches. We merely remain in Him and fruit will come. May we stay close to Jesus. May we be connected to Him. Not just when we feel like it, but all the time. Our connectedness to Jesus brings Him glory, and that would be enough. But, isn't it just like Jesus to care so deeply for us, that our connectedness to Him benefits us, as well? When we remain in His love, when we stay connected to Jesus, we find great joy that is complete. May each of you be filled with JOY as you remain in Jesus, our true Vine.

Lesson 7: Who is Jesus?

Pray

Jesus, please show me through your Word today who you are. Fill me with thoughts of you only, right now. I want to know you.

Read

John 11:1-44; John 20

Write

Journal anything that speaks to you or jumps out at you from the passage, including any questions you might have.

_____
_____
_____
_____
_____
_____
_____
_____

Answer

1) Who does Jesus say He is?

2) Jesus heard Lazarus was sick, but He stayed where He was for two more days. Why did Jesus not go to Lazarus sooner? (vs. 4, 15, 40, 42)

3) Lazarus' sisters, Martha and Mary, both had the same reaction when they saw Jesus. What did they say to Him?

4) Read the other accounts of Jesus' resurrection (Matthew 28:1-7, Mark 16:1-6, Luke 24:1-8). These three disciples tell that an angel appeared at Jesus' tomb, proclaiming that "He is not here. He has _____."

Reflect

Jesus loved Lazarus, Mary, and Martha. They were his friends. Yet, when He heard that Lazarus was sick, He chose not to go to him right away. Many knew that if Jesus showed up during Lazarus' illness, He would be able to heal his friend. He had already proven His power over sickness. But, this time was different. This time, Jesus planned to show He has power over death. Why?

His purpose was twofold – for His glory (11:4), and so that we might believe (11:14). Jesus let his friend die, not in vain, but for a purpose.

Fast forward to His own death. Jesus died, not in vain, but for a purpose. Jesus gave up His own life for a purpose: the greatest purpose of all time. Jesus died to set us free, to pay our price, to redeem us from our own destructive ways. And, unlike Lazarus, who needed someone else to raise him from the dead, Jesus needed no one else. He raised Himself from the dead, showing His ultimate power over death.

When Jesus finally does show up at Lazarus' home, He makes a BIG statement – *I am the resurrection and the life. The one who believes in me will live, even though they die; and whoever lives by believing in me will never die.*

Jesus gives us earthly life – He is Creator of all things. But, more importantly, Jesus gives us eternal life. His death and resurrection is the most incredible act of love in all of history. It is the most incredible act of love in all of the future. It is the most incredible act of love for all time. May you know His love for you. And, may our hearts, our minds, and our mouths cry out as Martha did: *I believe that you [Jesus] are the Messiah, the Son of God, who is to come into the world!*

Lesson 8: Why did Jesus Come?

Pray

Jesus, please show me through your Word today why you came. Fill me with thoughts of you only, right now. I want to know more about your love for me.

Read

Luke 19:1-10; John 3:16-18

Write

Journal anything that speaks to you or jumps out at you from the passage, including any questions you might have.

_____

_____

_____

_____

_____

_____

_____

_____

Answer

1) According to Luke 19:1-10, why did Jesus come?

2) Jesus went to Zacchaeus' house, showing that He was willing to hang out with what kind of people?

3) According to John 3:16-18, why did Jesus come?

4) What is one reason Jesus did *not* come into the world?

5) What must we do in order to have eternal life?

Reflect

To the people watching to see what Jesus would do, it seemed scandalous that He would hang out in the house of a sinner. But, praise the Lord this is what He is willing to do, because that is exactly who we are. Jesus spoke clearly that day. He came to seek out and to save the lost. He came to find any in need of a Savior, inviting them to be in His presence. Jesus came to save out of His great love for us (John 3:16)!

We deserve condemnation. We deserve death because of our great sin. May you know today that Jesus came to give *not what we deserve*. Rather, He came to give that which we *do not deserve*. Jesus came to save, and to breathe life into those who deserve death. May we believe in His name, and cherish this gift forever.

Lesson 9: Why did Jesus Come?

Pray

Jesus, please show me through your Word today why you came. Fill me with thoughts of you only, right now. I want to know more about your love for me.

Read

John 2:1-11

Write

Journal anything that speaks to you or jumps out at you from the passage, including any questions you might have.

_____

_____

_____

_____

_____

_____

_____

_____

Answer

1) Do you know which miracle of Jesus' this was?

2) Why did Jesus perform this miracle?

3) Based on your answer to Question 2, why did Jesus come?

Reflect

Turning water into wine at a wedding feast was Jesus' first miracle. It was the first of many. In Psalm 19, David penned these words: *The heavens declare the glory of God; the skies proclaim the work of his hands. Day after day they pour forth speech; night after night they reveal knowledge.*

Until Jesus came to our earth, it was creation revealing the glory of God.

Re-read John 2:11.

Enter Jesus. Now there was One performing signs and wonders on this earth, all over the place, things only God Himself could do. Jesus came to reveal the glory of God. Jesus came to reveal His own glory.

Look around you. See the glory of our Lord, revealed in His creation, as you watch the sunset or look at the mountains. Soak it in. Know that His creation proclaims His glory. Remember that everything Jesus did loudly proclaimed the glory of the Lord. Now, may we proclaim His glory until the day of His return!

Lesson 10: Why did Jesus Come?

Pray

Jesus, please show me through your Word today why you came. Fill me with thoughts of you only, right now. I want to know more about your love for me.

Read

Colossians 1:13-23

Write

Journal anything that speaks to you or jumps out at you from the passage, including any questions you might have.

_____

_____

_____

_____

_____

_____

_____

_____

Answer

1) In vs. 13-14, three reasons are mentioned as to why Jesus came. What are they?

2) Why were all things created?

3) What does Christ have over everything?

4) In vs. 22, two reasons are given as to why Jesus came. What are they?

Reflect

This passage isn't very long, but it is so full. Simply put, Jesus came to rescue us, to redeem us, to forgive us, to reconcile us, to present us as holy and without blemish.

Are you with me? Are you reading this? Is this sinking in?

Let's read that again. Only this time, put your own name in the place of "us" (I'll put mine, you replace mine with yours).

Jesus came to rescue Becky, to redeem Becky, to forgive Becky, to reconcile Becky, to present Becky as holy and without blemish.

Wow! I am so far from holy and without blemish, but this is what He came to do for me. This is what he came to do for you. We could not rescue ourselves. We could not redeem ourselves. We could not forgive ourselves. We could not reconcile ourselves. We cannot live holy lives, without blemish. However, because of the work of Jesus, we *are* rescued, redeemed, forgiven, reconciled, holy, and without blemish.

May we feel loved, and treasured, and cherished by Jesus today. May we believe these words of Scripture. May we know that He came to do these things (and so much more) on our behalf.

Lesson 11: Why did Jesus Come?

Pray

Jesus, please show me through your Word today why you came. Fill me with thoughts of you only, right now. I want to know more about your love for me.

Read

Matthew 20:20-28; John 13:1-17

Write

Journal anything that speaks to you or jumps out at you from the passage, including any questions you might have.

_____

_____

_____

_____

_____

_____

_____

_____

Answer

1) Like the sons of Zebedee, what do we often seek?

2) According to the passage in Matthew, why did Jesus come?

3) In what way did Jesus serve His disciples?

4) Why did Peter not want Jesus to wash his feet?

Reflect

How much I am like those sons of Zebedee, wanting to be honored, desiring to be great among men. When I look only to the things of this life, I truly believe this would fill me.

Jesus has something else to say, turning everything on its head, as He so often does. Here he tells His disciples that in order to be great, they must serve. Want to be first? Be a slave. He not only tells them to serve, He shows them how to serve. The Son of God humbles Himself and washes the disgusting, dirty feet of those He loves.

Scripture is clear. The God of the universe left His honored position in glory and entered our lowly home in order to serve out of love for us. May we see His glory and His humility. May we open our hands and our hearts to embrace that our Jesus - fully-God, deserving of honor and glory - came to serve.

Lesson 12: How do I Respond?

Pray

Jesus, I know who you are. I know why you came. Now, show me through your Word today what my response should be.

Read

Mark 12:28-31; John 13:34-35; John 15:12-17

Write

Journal anything that speaks to you or jumps out at you from the passage, including any questions you might have.

_____

_____

_____

_____

_____

_____

_____

_____

Answer

1) According to Jesus, which commandment is the most important?

2) Also according to Jesus, which commandment is the second most important?

3) What command did Jesus give us?

4) How will others know that we are Jesus' followers?

5) What is proof of the greatest love?

Reflect

Here is where it starts – we are to love the Lord, and love others.

It seems simple, yet it isn't.

But, love is the most important response we are to have. Jesus entered our world out of His great love for us. We are to love Him in return, and we are to love one another. This is not a request that Jesus makes. He does not timidly ask us to come alongside, and join Him in loving God and loving others. He *commands* us to do so. He calls us to this great work, knowing that love is what transforms. His love transforms our hearts and our lives.

Jesus loved us enough to lay down His life for us. We owe our very lives to Him, and He asks that we start with love. May we love Him and love others well today. May we rely on His love in order that our love might transform the world.

Discuss

How can I love the Lord well?

How can I love others well?

What are some specific ways I can show love at home, at school, at church, at work, in my neighborhood, in my community, and in the world?

Lesson 13: How do I Respond?

Pray

Jesus, I know who you are. I know why you came. Now, show me through your Word today what my response should be.

Read

2 Corinthians 5:15-21

Write

Journal anything that speaks to you or jumps out at you from the passage, including any questions you might have.

_____
_____
_____
_____
_____
_____
_____
_____

Answer

1) Since Jesus died for us, what should our response be? (vs. 15)

2) If we are in Christ (if we know Him and love Him), what are we? (vs. 17)

3) What ministry has God given to us? (vs. 18)

4) God has reconciled us to Himself, which means He does not do what? (vs. 19)

5) If we believe Jesus is who He says He is and did what He said He came to do, then what are we? (vs. 21)

Reflect

Once again, we come back to the fact that Jesus died for us. This is the heart of the gospel. His death and resurrection made a way for us when there was no way. He breathed life into us, and because of that, we are called to something very different. We are called away from living for ourselves, and into living for the One who gave His life for us. His death and resurrection created newness in us. His death and resurrection reconciled us to God, so part of our newness is a new calling, a new ministry – the ministry of reconciliation.

Reconciliation is the restoration of relationship. Sin destroyed our relationship with the Lord. Jesus restored our relationship with the Lord. Now we, by His grace and with His help, seek to be restorers of relationships in our world, caring deeply for those around us, desiring that they see His love for them in us.

May we live as new creations, leaning into Jesus, trusting Him to work in us and through us. May we step out into the ministry of reconciliation, showing His love to those around us, seeking to be relationship-restorers, instead of relationship-destroyers. May we show off for Him, shining His light, having His heart for others. May we be His ambassadors (vs.20), His representatives, His hands and feet. This fallen, hurting world needs you and me, because this fallen, hurting world needs Jesus.

Discuss

How can I be Jesus to a fallen, hurting world?

Lesson 14: How do I Respond?

Pray

Jesus, I know who you are. I know why you came. Now, show me through your Word today what my response should be.

Read

James 1:22-27; John 21

Write

Journal anything that speaks to you or jumps out at you from the passage, including any questions you might have.

_____
_____
_____
_____
_____
_____
_____
_____

Answer

1) What should we not do with the Word of God? What should we do instead?

2) Do we benefit by being doers of the Word? If so, how?

3) What does the Lord desire for us to do with our religion?

4) What is John's (the disciple Jesus loved) response when he realizes it is Jesus standing on the shore?

5) What does Jesus tell Peter to do?

Reflect

The Lord Jesus has been faithful these last two weeks to meet us in His Word, to show us who He is, and to reveal to us why He came. He has lovingly reminded us what our role is, showing us that we are to love Him and love others. He has reminded us that we are to live for Him, not for ourselves, caring deeply for those around us, seeking to restore relationships, showing the love He has for our fallen, hurting world.

So, today, we wrap all of this up with two passages that show us how to live for Him. We know who He is. We know why He came. Therefore, how should we respond? What should we do?

First, we should be doers of His Word! What an analogy we are given in James 1:23-24! If we just listen to (or read) God's Word without doing what it says, we will forget everything. It does no good for us or anyone else. His Word is life-giving, it is freedom, and if we do what it says to do, blessing comes in the doing.

Second, religion without works to back it up is meaningless. When we know and love Jesus, we will live differently. We will care for the orphan and the widow, loving the poor, the lonely, the needy, as Jesus did when He walked the earth. We will seek to keep ourselves from being polluted by the world. This is hard! The world is actually not our friend. Satan seeks to use it to steal, kill, and destroy. If we are not doers of His Word, we are easily tossed around, swaying in the wind, not knowing (or caring) which way we should go.

Here's some good news, though...

We all struggle. We all fail, and fall, and flounder.

Enter Peter, the rock on which Christ built His Church (Matthew 16:18). He walked closely with Jesus, knowing Him, loving Him, serving Him. Yet, he failed, and fell, and floundered. He denied even knowing His dear friend and brother, the Savior of the world (read Luke 22:54-62 to find out more). He deserved to be cut off from Jesus, but don't we know by now that Christ does not treat us as our sins deserve?

Jesus restored Peter. He also called him out to something different. He restores us, and calls us out to something different, as well. As with Peter, if we love Jesus, we are called to feed His lambs, to take care of His sheep, and to follow Him.

If we are doers of His Word, then we will seek to live as Jesus lived. We will care for the orphan, the widow, the lonely, the poor, the outcast, the picked-on, the unlovable. We will feed and care for His people. We will follow Him. We will not do these things perfectly, but with His help, we will do these things. By God's grace, may we seek to live as Jesus lived. He came not to be served, but to serve. May we seek to serve Him and serve others with our lives.

Discuss

How can I serve others today?

How can I serve others every day?

Made in United States
North Haven, CT
16 July 2024

54893772R00022